This book is from:

_____

To you:

_____

Jojo
the playground buddy

Jojo the playground buddy

By Abigail Adeyanju

Illustrated by Da. Marton

Jojo the playground buddy

All rights reserved. No part of this book may be used or reproduced in any manner whatsoever without prior written consent of the author, except as provided by the United States of America copyright law.

ISBN: 9798717290562

AUTHOR: Abigail Adeyanju
ILLUSTRATED by Da Marton
damarton.artstation.com

Author's dedication

Firstly, I dedicate this book to my nephew Joel. A kind-hearted extremely clever boy who has always shown courage and strength in everything he does and every situation he finds himself. Thank you for inspiring me.

I also dedicate this book to all my nieces, nephews and god-children who find themselves navigating relationships and experiences during their daily school life most especially amongst classroom peers…. Be strong, courageous, and always treat others as you would wish to be treated. "choose to be the light".

Finally, I would like to dedicate this book to my sons; Timi and Jensen. Both who have taught me so many lessons during my parenting journey. You are both the reason why I practice and advocate emotional intelligent parenting. Supporting you both navigate your daily challenges and successes has given me the chance to help other parents on their journey too.

I look forward to going to school because my day starts with a bicycle ride through the park.

School is mostly fun for me because I get to learn fun stuff.

The best time of my school day is 'break time'.

Playground time!!

The playground is where it is ok to have boys and girls in groups playing together

Playground time is my HAPPY time...

Sometimes, the playground makes me SAD. I know the playground sometimes makes you SAD too.

Some words are so hurtful that it makes you feel like you have just been kicked in the stomach and your stomach is in knots.

Hurtful words make people feel sad and teary.

Always remember that the playground should make you feel safe and happy.

The playground is a place where everyone should RESPECT each other.

The playground should always be a FRIENDLY and HAPPY space for all.

A place where you should 'BE YOURSELF'.

If anyone upsets you, or you feel LONELY and ANXIOUS about anything, always speak to a teacher or adult.

You can also ask for a playground buddy.

Someone like Jojo!

This will make you feel better.

A playground buddy is kind
friendly
respectful
helpful
always listens
and makes you feel good 😊

Why?

Author's note

Every child is a social and emotional being.

Children expect to feel comfortable in school, especially on the playground. Unfortunately, the playground has also been identified as a place where children experience intimidation, discrimination, and humiliation in the form of bullying.

This book aims to remind children that the playground is designed to be a fun place for all. If the need arises, you can use your voice by either speaking to a teacher or simply requesting for a playground buddy from an adult/playground supervisor.

This book also encourages the child who is in the position to speak up and speak out against playground bullies to use their voice for good whilst showing empathy for others.

Abigail Adeyanju is a certified emotional intelligence practitioner, educator and trainer based in London. She runs one-on-one and group Socio-Emotional Learning (SEL) sessions and workshop for children.

Printed in Great Britain
by Amazon

66664126R00017